A GOOD-NIGHT

IN AMERICA

Charles R Castle Jr

First Printing, May 2017

ISBN-13: 978-1545588161
ISBN-10: 1545588163

Cover Photo: by author - toward Kesey Square, Eugene, Oregon

To June:
I hope a few of these
poems speak to you as
fondly as Sandra speaks
of you.
                Charles

In Gratitude

All the attendant poets

Sandra – for loving inspiration
Margaret – for encouragement
proofing & showing up for coffee
Deb Amber McKenzie Danielle
for everything

I am a work in process.
These are the words I use to keep my heart open.

In a world always on the verge,
you start where you are.
Perhaps this is how a new universe
is created with a word.

Table of Contents

MINUTES HOURS AND DAYS

THESE THOUGHTS OF YOU

A GOOD-NIGHT IN AMERICA

WHAT I NEVER THOUGHT TO IMAGINE

Minutes Hours and Days

Minutes Hours and Days

Let's lay our words out one by one
like minutes hours and days
and pass our time in simple rhyme
like children here at play
Let's raise our swords to vanquish foes
and cast our demons down
and bring our angels back to life
and then go paint the town

With dark phrases and bright ideas
let's run and tell our stories
post metaphors on every door
with glowing allegories
And when our lives are over
and our poems are flower beds
may their fragrance ever linger
and continue to be read

Let's lay our words out one by one
like weeks and months and years
And while the whole world worries by
let's write away our fears
Let's raise our pens to all our friends
who with us here still play
to write our words out one by one
like minutes hours and days

We'll worry not if we're forgot
in decades soon to come
for all these words we'll ever share
our souls remember some
And they'll be free for all to see
so this to you I say
write your words out one by one
like minutes hours and days.

7/7/2016

Swimming the Parting Waters

I cook the packaged rice

I salt the simmered fish

What feeds the heart and soul

Fills no single dish

The heavens call to all men

Oceans part for no one here

To reach those far off shores

We swim our seas of fear

She taught her heart to fly

Where once she had no wings

Now let pass through its veil

A world of lighter things

When every dream comes true

When we grant love's every wish

I cook the packaged rice

I salt the simmered fish

4/22/2017

The Poetry of Dust

A book spilled from a shelf
splayed open on the floor
Notes in disarray
Old pencils with their erasers dry
The room is an echo of words

To hear them
make the sound of a finger
smudging through gathered dust
in the narrow space between
upright books and the falling edge

To hear them
make the sound of coffee at dawn
or the sound of a memory;
the lingering coolness
of a lover's kiss on your neck

There is poetry in dust
that stands in light
and dust in poetry
that falls to silence

Go places birds
will sit on your shoulders
and listen
for echoes

8/3/2016

All the Places We Are Lost

In the alfalfa-field June
of calves and foals
they married their ranch-farm lands   She
with her honey-parted hips   He
with his bone-dog bee   They were
summer's flower bed   They were
winter's hive afire   They were
coyote-howling nights and sweet-dripping days

Then came lean locust years and empty-nursery mornings
and in the ache that followed   the withheld words   the
question   Who was barren   Who was the hollow seed

He   withdrew to thunder's distance
digging back-forty fences   while   she
wandered the empty lofts   alone

She called out in her cow-town voice
How could you leave me no midnight horse to ride My
wild-mare heart is broken and you hold its reins at a
mother's rusted gate

His wind-echo chest stampeding fears
in his herded heart   he answered
In this dry winter you are the alpine springs I cannot reach
You are the high country and all the places I am lost Where
can I go not desert beneath frost on a father's fallow field

On the ranch-farm pastures lay the abandoned bales of what
he could not say and she could not hear   Below ridgelines
they walk the lame horses where waters will flow again when
the smell of alfalfa calls them home
10/8/2016

The Weight of Bones and Ice

In thick cold fog
we walk the ponds   where herons nest
in March.   The trees are silhouettes of
bones   laid hard on winter's face.   And
with their barren hands to heaven,   ice-
encrusted fingers hold in bleak dominion
the brittle land.

Beneath the branch
arched   heavy hung, a solitary bird endures
the frozen edge. There we too, hunched stiff-
shouldered, yearn for sun. We labor brighter
images   and from spring's new kingdom   call
the tinted buds

to hatch their leaves
and stir in warmer wind   their April wings.   Yet
this view the winter weighs on last year's scales,
the mind's eye   fogged and
ladened by   the distance.

12/21/2016

All These Lakes Gone Dry

more often now
i try to remember where
the small boy and the dark water trout
swam knee-deep together

where skunk cabbage afternoons
bloomed from lady slipper mornings

and where something big
like an uncaught dream
cruised just beneath the surface
waiting to feed

2/10/2016

What Falls Fastest

Falls hardest
What floats lightest
Last longest
What shows weakest
Bends farthest
What moves silent
Moves strongest

4/28/2017

Working a Prompt

A yellow M&M
picked from the floor.
Its candied shell is cracked.
It sits on the arm
of a red loveseat,
a little old, a little worn.

Wives and girlfriends,
my grown children,
friends and strangers
have all sat there.

A red loveseat,
concaved cushions
no longer firm,
sits under
a yellow M&M.
Its candied shell is cracked.

It would melt in your mouth.
It would melt in your hand.

Wives and girlfriends,
my grown children,
friends and strangers
have all sat there.

4/8/2017

Singing Down the Mountain

Wake up, your time has come
The wind is crisp off the Sisters
You are on the downward side to the sea
These rivers and you have become one destination
Your closest companions are your hands about your eyes
These valleys are themselves songs
and you sing through them
You are in them as rain, moonlight and tears
The landscape is your long sought dream
You are as full as you are

My hands are cupped
I listen for you

11/10/2016

Hunting Among the Bones

The obsidian arrowheads
Found among the bones and ash
Of paleo-poetic campfires
Can still be made into weapons
To bring down prey

11/6/2017

Cupping Water

What do I really know
These hands are the very clay
I use to shape the world
I could dismantle their bones
and still not see where
the blood in them is born

Chemistry is not insight
into the heart
Eyes see by belief
Ears are deaf to what they
have no design to hear
Even my mind is divided
its full sky unknown to me

Still we try for more
and all these blood-fed words
are the bones of wings
I piece together

I have the need to know
why I cup water in my hands
and see myself
in you

10/9/2016

Anthropic's Tavern

Probability waves at the waitress
He's just a customer who hasn't ordered yet
Certainty orders the same old thing every day
He's particular about addin' up the bill
Creation is a short-order cook workin' a seven day week
Time is the illusion we use to read the menu
We always get what we ask for
I'm thinkin' of askin' for the Blue Plate Special
I'm thinkin' Happy Hour is just a different
seat at the bar and I'm about to move

2/19/2017

The Sound of When

Mostly I don't mind silence
Mostly I don't mind if it rains
Mostly I get on with life
Mostly I'm up before dawn

Sometimes I get big ideas
Sometimes I look in dark places
Sometimes answers hide in plain sight
Sometimes it's best to do nothing

Always I wonder why it's like this
Always I think there's more
Always I listen for beginnings
Always night bends into morning

Today I sit in the quiet
Today I give light attention
Today is a *now* sound to feel
Today sings brightly through my fingers

2/19/2017

Clem's Nails

Pounding the nails Clem left me,
I'm reminded to use the tools I have.
We're months from a dedication.
I'm Site Super building for Habitat
and a family of four, with one due
in spring, has been waiting two years.
It's slow going with a volunteer crew.
Some can't climb the ladders.

The windows still need caulking, yet the roof
is sheathed and felted. The contractors
keep their own schedules, but they support
the cause and cut us a break on the bill.
On this morning with November's geese above,
it's not yesterday's sky I tack the ridge
vents under. I'm over sixty and thankful
for the work.

Long 2 x 4 bracing and scrap lumber stacked,
my pouch pockets carry the pulled bent nails.
The sixteen penny sinkers, vinyl-coated,
cat's paw out hot to the touch.
No effort will make them straight again,
yet they might still serve if the big box
goes empty.

1/22/2017

Bathroom Floor

The vinyl goes down on Thursday
There will be no seam
Use double-sided tape against the tub
and under the door
All the edges against the walls float free
Molding will cover the space for expansion
Give it time to lay flat

3/7/2017

In My House of Corners

I took the rug and raised the edge
The moment held me there
My broom was poised above the pile
Of my debris of years
Regrets of sand, a dust of hurts
A cloud of settled slights

I am in my age of cleaning
To let resentments go
And let a light refresh
The darker places I have known

How do we pass through life
When hard feelings are the clay
We track into our holiness
And let harden all our days

4/15/2017

Not the Same as Being by the Sea

What we are is not the same as what we're made of.

Just as music is not the parts of a piano, or the bow

and string are not the vibration of a minor key.

And what we are is not the same as all our parts,

as our ears know no difference between a symphony

and a baby's cry, or our fingers know no difference

between sun-warmed silk and our lover's skin.

What we are is not the same as what we're made of.

Just as a stack of moments is not a lifetime, or childhood

is not a child yet reminds of moments of a child.

Or as losing a lover, or a child, is not the same as an empty

bed, a quiet house, or a stack of photographs. Or as standing

at the edge of the ocean, face wet with wind, is not the same

as a face wet with tears.

No, what we are is not the same as what we're made of,

as love is not the same as loving, as a heart broken

is not the same as a failing heart, or as holding a child's hand

is not the same as holding a box of ashes by the sea.

2/26/2017

Black Crow on Snow

I scatter my father's ashes
Dark feathers flayed
dusted white
loss intends no small favors
Stiff as bones
stuck in my throat
hard as letting go

Black crow on snow
I scatter my father's ashes
Day's bleak tongue
night's vacant eye
tucked beneath
a broken wing
An old man's hand
I come too late to hold

Black crow on snow
I scatter my father's ashes
Sky's leaden blanket
weighs as weather
Time like snow falls
in heavy layers
deep on mourning
as unsaid prayers

Black crow on snow
I scatter my father's ashes
Does knowing lessen
life's affliction
or grief foreshorten
A winter's year
into a decade
so silent passes

3/20/2017

On Winter's Death

winter dies
I dream my father's
in the garden

winter dies
my mother hears
next year's crickets

winter dies
spring slips past
headstone flowers

8/23/2015

These Thoughts of You

What Here I Grow

When it all comes around again
it's the simple things that matter
the fire in winter
the path to the garden
the first spring peas

When it all comes around
it's the place you rest your heart
in someone's hands that matters
It's the touch that says   yes
we can be both frost and fire
and still find ourselves together
in the morning

This is when
the sun begs the world
to sprout itself
and the heart to hatch
from January's shell of ice
to turn green
turn out new leaves and climb vine-like
all love's possibilities and bloom

Warm hands
in their green promise
nurture a new season
to stir and call
from melting snow
the hum of bees
and what here I grow
for you now

1/5/2017

These Thoughts of You

It's the color of the sky in the morning
how it transitions from baby blue to something like pink
where it meets the earth with a color less like haze
than the impression of hair above a woman's lip
that makes you want to kiss them both

It's the way these colors of the sky blend together
raising this longing in me to be in your bed on this morning
when you and I are so far apart

Even the morning's full moon regrets the distance home
where the sun is reluctant to rise
wishing it did not have to wake me
from these thoughts of you

6/22/2016

In the Mood of Gray

I tend to lean on   memories,   cloudy skies
and similes. Comfortable   days   are like faded jeans
and old sweaters.   I never met   a shade of gray
sky   I did   not like.   Rough weather
soothes   these feelings   you left me.
The fewer   words   the better.

When love comes   around   I meet it at the door.
Wipe   your feet,   come on in.
Your coat becomes   you   like the rain becomes
this November night. Shake it out.   Sit by the fire.
I have whatever you   need.   all the visits you stayed
over, this woodstove holds as old   flames and ashes

what we burned well in winters long gone. I've some
thing warm in the   oven.   Tea takes its own time.
The cups are   in the cupboard.   My heart's
where it's always been.   I see you've   been crying.
Your tears will never   put out   this fire
between   us.

I fixed the rocking leg   on the broken   chair.   I cut
from the seasoned   hardwood of   our youth.
This is the season for   sharing love   and steadfast
metaphors. Sleep   under   these blankets
of mine when you have   the heart. I'm going to bed,
it's getting   late.

10/3/2016

There's No Reason

Come dance with me,
there's no reason we can't be in love.
The moon is above
and the sun will come up with the day.

We've only these years, fewer than
fingers and toes.
It's the fourth of July, let's be wild like
the buck and the doe
and outrun our past and lie down at last
in the snow.
By the first of the year we'll have melted our fears,
don't you know.

And have left there instead the impression of
lovers in bed.
We'll have flowed from that place like water to space,
beings divine.
You'll let go into me, I'll let go into you,
we'll leave nothing behind.
There's no reason we can't be in love,
no one will mind.

When there's no more to say, let's dance it away.
The moon is above
and the sun will come up with the day.

7/4/2016

Render Unto Caesar

In affairs of the heart
what sets the strong apart

Those hard-fought battles lost
who estimates the cost

I did not know when I pleased her
what I would render unto Caesar

or the freedom I'd leave there
when love and need I'd not compared

In the blood that flows our veins
hides chemistry for joy and pain

12/7/2016

My Dream of Another Spring

When it comes,
that last day,
that quiet night, let us be gardens
of tender flowers and smiles
of the softest thorn-pain and new roses.
And let us pick them for each other,
especially,
yet for the children, mostly.

Let us pick them for everyone
we have ever loved, especially.
And for those who still love us, mostly.

And when there is nothing left to forgive,
save forgiving ourselves our thorns,
may it be done by grace.
Gardens too must forgive themselves
for what they could not grow.

Let us be gardens, you and I,
for each other and all
and I will remember your sun-deep soil
and the leaves you caressed me with.
And perhaps you will remember
I was the sun shining over you whispering
grow the world with all these seeds
and love me green again.

So when it comes
let us both be green in our softest tears,
in our deepest soil and in our sun-bright
rooted hearts
and I will hold for you
my dream of another spring.

8/25/2016

These Tortured Skies

I ask the harrowed wind
to lend me its song.
It offers nothing
but this breath of mine.

I ask the unblinking world
to release these eyes.
It grants nothing save
to break my heart with sight.

I ask for the night bird's flight.
Its dragon-scaled feathers
tear my wings
yet it lifts me and I soar.

Fly with me, sing. Share
this song of sunset's tears.
Sing the night I walk
praying to you
and I will sing the day
you run loving to me.

Whisper the words only you know
and I will sing them back to you.
Together we will face
these ruby-tortured skies
till night's fire-breath angel
returns our chorus home.

9/18/2016

Desire Speaks When
She Sleepwalks

Love sings in the shower
songs more expressive than words
They sing a passion
to change the world
We illuminate the darkness
with our eyes closed in just
the right way
Night's bright light can awaken
new emotions above a bed
These morning sheets
are laughing in their dreams

Desire speaks when she sleepwalks
There are things I would have her say again

10/22/2016

The Mother's Gift

Dark was the loss that she embraced
like widow's lace hung 'bout her face
woven from a lover's slight
with stitches torn and re-sewn tight

From mother's words she patterned more
and wove the clothes her children wore
Old garments passed as something blue
that severed vows between the two

Who can expose what deeply lives
to learn to love and self-forgive
and wed the two and so release
both bride and groom to find their peace

Where love's concerned, it's what we learn
and what we sew is what we earn
We're cut from cloth our bloodline weaves
We run from home   We seldom leave

12/31/2016

Loving Relatively

Where are the pieces hidden
of the things we want and need
I have pulled apart family
I have pulled apart friends
I have pulled apart lovers
I have tried to pull apart love
only to find it had no parts

From quantum science we learn
there is only interconnectedness

How do I reconcile living
when on this morning
I seem to wake alone
and why
I feel this particular longing
in this singular place in me
and why
you seem so far away

3/11/2017

Hard to Tell

Some women hold love like a blessing
Some wield it like a witch's spell
Some say love can last forever
I think it's just so hard to tell

Some women fight like martyrs
Some command and some rebel
For some love's a war of giving
I think it's just so hard to tell

Some display their souls as mirrors
Some reveal their souls as wells
All reflections are deceiving
I think it's just so hard to tell

Some women rent their love for pennies
Some own the golden place it dwells
Some say poems are cheap diversions
I think it's just so hard to tell

3/11/2017

Darkness Falls

We went down to Darkness Falls to hear the water sing
We walked paths by evergreens that drew from deeper springs
My love and I ran hand in hand like feathers on a breeze
To hear the songs of nightingales nesting in the trees

The mountain shed its mantled head, the valley called it down
It spread the canyon with its flood and made a joyful sound
Like a bed the deep green moss around the water lay
As soft as skin it called us in, the pool below the spray

A gentle mist held hands to eyes as darkness sang to night
And we undressed on summer's lips that kissed the fading light
We submerged to depths as deep as any star-filled sky
To be blessed like falling stars since like them we could fly

We too fell from heaven's edge as night spent into day
To fade from bliss with one last kiss when love had had its way
What desire calls in time expires and passion called must too
For love must wake within to last and prove that it is true

We woke by dawn to Darkness Falls where silent questions grew
What we never thought to ask ourselves while dancing on the dew
Why water flows forever, yet love is fickle by the day
And if nightingales regret their songs when lovers fly away

3/6/2017

A Good-night in America

To the Ones Who Know

You can paint a coat of color
over all these things
You can get in bed with evil
and his seven kings
Or you can break a vow of silence
to command the wind
when Nero burns the cities
with his violin

When the scholars High and Holy
will stand no ground
and the voices in the choir
will sing no sound
someone paves the roadways
and draws the maps
that lead us to a wasteland
where they've set the traps

When the brown shirts wear the colors
of the red white and blue
And the people drink the Kool-Aid
what does freedom do
History repeats itself
but who reads books
and the ones that know ain't speakin'
when the rest are crooks

A cross with an agenda
wields a racist flame
A court rules for abuse
and it's a deadly game
If a dollar buys a sound-bite
that's believed as truth
freedom's just a slave
inside a voting booth

11/9/2016

Circus Trial for the American Dream

Hear ye, hear ye, hear ye, all rise.
A new hangin' judge will be seated soon.
Genuflect, cross your heart,
give a Hitler high-five to the flag.
This is our American dream life
and we are all on trial tonight.
Smart money says the jury's been bought.

It's a three-ringed circus under the big top -
executive, legislative and judicial,
a carnival atmosphere with no shortage of scary clowns.
Step right up, buy your ticket from the tiny strongman,
the one wearin' nothin' but a black satin cape, an AK 47
and his amphetamine smile.

We all want to live somewhere we can be free.
Mine is in this right hemisphere.
This is where I work, the place I call home.
Right here, yes sir,
a dark place on a small stage
under blue lights in a smoky haze.
Is that cabaret music I hear?

My co-conspirators and I are mighty glad you came tonight.
Take a seat on these pine-pitch benches.
OSHA regulations require I wear this mask
with its red mechanical tongue, glass doll eyes and
rouged corporate logo cheeks.
I'm slurrin' my words 'cause I drank the Kool-Aid.
It tastes like gratuitous sex, tomorrow's worries
and every moment's apprehensions.
These are things that could make a man angry
if he could afford the luxury,
if he wasn't workin' unpaid overtime
for fabricated wars, criminal bailouts and
nefarious nightmares that keep him awake at night.

But that ain't me, I'm patriotic and I do what I'm told.

I put in my time, I did it in my sleep.
I was a creative type, I manufactured dreams.
I rewrote history, I sold it back as truth.
I wrote sermons for a salvation you could buy on lay-away.
I married church and state and you paid for the wedding.
I invented the enemies your sons and daughters died fighting.
I read the evening news of coups and assassinations
that served the bottom line, the party line or the toe-the-line.
I made the TV ads with Kama Sutra poses superimposed
on new cars, all moving in slow motion.
I gave you that funny feelin',
that urge to buy something you didn't need.
I packaged the idols for Christmas.
I counted down the New Year that never came.

I'm retired now and it all seems so far away.
There was a time we had an urge for more
than just a bigger market share.
There was a time we dreamed
of something better for each other,
but then what are such dreams worth?

So ladies and gentlemen,
welcome to the trial of the century.
Silence your phones, no pictures please,
the video will be posted by morning.
The jury is seated, the stage is set.
The red, white and blue curtains open.
See the torch-bearing woman sawn in half,
the faceless magician with his bloody hands.
Who do the gloves fit now?
Take a deep breath,
don't blink.

12/17/2016

A Good-night in America

Sleepless street lights, parking lots and all night laundries

Midnight is a memory 2AM has forgotten   Sidewalks curled up

like possums playing dead Ghosts of forgotten people

wrap themselves in the dreams of better times and find no rest

It's only the stones in their shoes that inspire them to walk

the nights alone Life's a one-way street anyway you look at it

All across these black lawns crushing sameness has been spread

like weed killer The mown blades of grass bleed mediocrity

Leaves on trees are limp like tears the branches wish

they could forget Even the stars find no will to live in this sky

tonight Demons of complacency pace these sweating rooftops

and tear their hair There are trained seals in these dry ditches

that have not been fed They wish nothing but to die with the last

salmon and return to the sea

The circus is in town for another four years and all these empty

cars on all these empty streets must perform for the first show

at dawn On the fairgrounds it's so quiet you can hear the pain

of the last living elephant It's so quiet you can hear the bearded

fortune teller light her first cigar of the day Her lover the dwarf

soldier stands erect by the red white and blue carnival cannon

preparing to be fodder   again   War is always in the cards

Coffee has no soul at this hour Sleepwalkers wander

down by the river every night about now It's a river damned

at dark to save water for those who can afford it

Those folks don't live anywhere near here

Under a small tent a revival meeting is in progress

The communion is breaking up the parched bodies of the poor

New recruits line up for induction seeking salvation in the Army

They salute three meals a day The uniformed preacher

holds up lyrics on cardboard signs The laid-off carnies

and the homeless are crooning the Sinner's Serenade

and other patriotic hymns to happiness

Bipolar twins on crutches are singing backup

Down in the river's holy ghost knee-deep and naked

descendents of pioneers are being baptize for the third time

The old ways don't take these days like they use to

At the fairgrounds in a bed of thieves there's a wet parting

The fortune teller lights the cannon fuse The cards

are laid down hard and the soldier's misfortune is set in stone

The sound of four more years of war tears open the day

The sweet smell of amnesia is in the air

It's a good-night to be alive in America

6/1/2016

American Hospital Emergency

Brain tumor eyes and cold black coffee
the night shift silent ghosts depart
Soft-souled nurses in their practical shoes drip intravenous
hope into the small hours
Elevator-nights and subdued lighting illuminate lone vigils
and families-in-waiting
Sad stories can be read in the patterns on pillows
brought from home
Abandoned mops and cleaning carts reach out to unseen voices
down dark hallways Time passes but it does not move
Impatient sleep cries out in all the rooms that cannot rest
It's just another night as healthcare tries to heal itself

The process starts up early There's a schedule to keep
Through tear-streaked windows morning waits on the skyline
with the weather
A mammoth building expansion's steam-shovel hands directs
construction cranes and concrete dump trucks
A bone-cracking parking structure pile driver beats the day awake
On the Cardio Unit all the heart monitors sync up within minutes
On Neuro migranes march to it beating their heads against walls
All the med carts cough up pills uncontrollably The chapel statues
pull cracked veils over their heads and pray
In the morgue draped bodies on wheeled gurneys pulsate to the beat
It's going to be a long day

In the old building it's business as usual
There are empty hallways where even the dead won't walk
The pipes leak a bad smell no one can identify
Whole wings are off limits
No one talks about it but we're all hearing the voices now
The psychiatrists and social workers have two-day hangovers
The top Neurosurgeon was found asleep in his third new
Lamborghini He'd been weeping

The voices aren't the worst of it something else is going on
The insurance companies have stopped answering their phones
Their message systems skip like old vinyl records
No one can get pre-approvals The CEOs haven't been seen in weeks
and there's a rumor someone skipped town after the bonuses were
paid

The radical reporter's been stalking staff in the alley since his mother
died   His malpractice appeal was dismissed in arbitration
Anonymous people are emailing him from the dark web
He'd buy a gun if he didn't think it would hurt his reputation

Meanwhile someone's grandmother got on the roof of the skybridge
between surgery and the business office
She's sitting naked in a rocking chair knitting baby blankets
Her surgery scars can be seen by the live-feed news The police
and EMTs are trying to talk her down but they're apprehensive
about the wired package taped under her chair
Framed pictures of her grandchildren are on display around her
She's doing it for them Unbeknownst to the parents
the kids are watching on social media
The Director of Public Affairs is massaging the message tenor and tone
She's passing out business cards She's got irons in the fire
Hospital Admin takes the back way out after the board meeting
There'll be late night calls to donors and investment managers

Construction stops sometime after dark
The rain falls hard
Morning will be just another day
coming soon enough

9/18/2016

Body in a Bathtub

Body in a bathtub
Bathtub bathtub
Body in a bathtub
Looks like mine

Freedom in a breadline
Dead dreams workin' overtime
Souls in jobs like strychnine
Looks like mine

Body in a church pew
Church pew church pew
Holy water overdue
Looks like mine

Hate preachin' bitter wine
Bad blood clottin' party lines
Reason bleeds on floors of crimes
Looks like mine

Body on the roadway
High as any sky say
Are you going my way
Looks like mine

Big Pharma pushin' dealer's dimes
People runnin' traffic signs
We're dyin' in our downtime
Looks like mine

Bodies on the playground
Assault guns shootin' children down
Bullet casing's sprayed around
Looks like mine

Poison in the waterlines
Babies needin' burial rhymes
Reachin' out for better times
Looks like mine

8/23/2016

Power's Privilege

When you were a boy
did you fly upon
the wind

or were you
tethered down by wealth
and all
your father's sins

Were you
taught that life was war
to kill
to keep from losing

or was it in your nature
and
the manner of
your choosing

12/12/2016

Jesus Saves the Big Banks

The second comin' was rolled out
after the bankers foreclosed on the churches.
They put Jesus on retainer to save the system.

He rode his private elevator from his office on the 64th floor
He had diamonds and gold on every finger.
In the lobby he told the angry people,
I'm a prophet with skin in the game.
The people stood firm sayin',
When you speak in tongues it's cuz you got nothin' to say.

There was a battle goin' on, it was dimes to dollars.
It was smoke and mirrors for an imaginary retirement.
It was *sign right here, it's only your soul* for a variable interest
rate and a second mortgage.
Jesus had a flock to tend.
Fleece 'em, sheep to the slaughter.

Jesus went into the Church of the Market.
He had sermons to improve the bottom line,
parables to make loan officers work longer hours
and sleep better at night.
He was shakin'things up.
He'd send out the memo Monday.
The banks were makin' too little profit off people
who couldn't pay their own way to heaven.
Credit was passé.
He'd embed their souls in plastic.

On the mean streets of suburbia
there was real money to be made.
Everyone would be nailed to a cross.

Let them beg for redemption this time.
Pulpits would collect on debt owed into the next life.
Altars would accept only the equity of a first born child.

Back in his office Jesus was signin' bonus checks
with other people's blood.
They kept that black ink in the vault by the barrel.
His pens were made from the bones of babies
the hospitals couldn't afford to bury.
Healthcare wasn't a birthright, everything had a cost
and a markup, even bein' born.

Down on the avenue
protestors were marchin' and carryin' signs.
The Father and the Holy Ghost led the chants and rants.
He'd had Dad voted off the corporate board.
You could buy anyone's faith for a percentage.
The Holy Ghost had been elusive
and always missed the meetings.
Hell, let security handle it.
Jesus shook his pen and went back to signing checks.
It was a good day to be a banker in America.

6/11/2016

Guthrie's Ghost Haunts Eugene

Woody rode in on the rails
He felt like heavy freight
He was dust-bowled and depressed
He was hitch-hiked
left high and dry on a cold wet night
It's a hard rain been fallin' lately
He looked for shelter under a bridge
He found fences around a land
once meant for you and me
He wondered what they protected
such a small patch of freedom there

Woody needed a shave
Woody needed a bath
Woody needed a bowl a' soup
and a bread line
A bed seemed too much to ask
with everyone sleepin'
No one sees ghosts these days
They sleep in the only graves we've left for them

Woody wandered onto Broadway
It was a hungry Saturday night in Eugene
He recognized all those gentle souls
he'd met on the highway to California
Busted farmers busted families
the busted-up and worse
They all said
"Howdy Woody it's been a real long time"
Woody looked around sayin'
"Don't seem like so much has changed"

Woody wished he could pay the union dues he owed
but the unions were busted up too
Right then the cops pushed through
sweepin' the streets and moved the whole shebang back
another block from the Bank of America

Woody said
"I remember when I could get a cup of coffee for a song
now I can't get one for a week's pay
How's a poor boy get by these days"
Someone strummed a chord on an old guitar
"Ah, that's a tune I recall
Glad the whole world aint dead
I've been seeing ghosts everywhere I go
It's been slim pickins'   hard places
empty faces   loud voices   few choices
little rhyme   and not much poetry
I been a long time ridin' a highway like a wave
It's been a big ocean I've sailed and seen
I've seen storms and angry times   but this . . .
this is a grapes of wrath of a new dimension
A wine of bile poured from the hearts of bitter men
Soul-starved souls who would eat their own children
to feed their timid faith
It's a middle class dust-bowl-of-debt
and the wind's just startin' to blow hard
This is a landslide you can feel on a Richter scale
We best leave the building while we still can
This house is comin' down"

Later   under familiar constellations
the small hours of morning hobo-ed up

to a rusted train going north
Woody stood waitin' for a son to rise
Lookin' east and west he saw nothin'
but oceans of desperation
He closed his eyes and a sea breeze
of sadness went right through him like a prayer
Over by the river of hope
on a pole above the House of Justice
an American flag tried to move

but it slept so ragged and faded
it couldn't even dream
It was bled-out and bone-tired from serving
special interests

Woody threw his pack over one shoulder
and moved toward the sound of a freight train whistle
He still remembered where the golden valley was hidden
and how far it was to get there by dawn
He felt a song rise up in him
He had nothin' left but to sing

8/8/2016

Finding
Cloven McGovern & Barnaby Bell

Cloven McGovern when he was five
Fell down a well and nearly died
His parents searched where he wasn't found
Where they didn't listen they heard no sound
Then they went home to feed the kids
There was nothing to say so no one did
What became of Cloven McGovern
No one was sure and no one discovered

When he was five Barnaby Bell
Got quite sick till he nearly got well
He went missing one day at school
His teachers swore by their golden rule
They had him down on all their lists
And if he was there he couldn't be missed
What became of Barnaby Bell
They thought they knew but they couldn't tell

It's not that people didn't care
Who finds the boy who isn't there

4/18/2017

In this Land We've Taken

If schools don't teach the story
Of the road that we have run
Will our children feel the burden
Of the things that we have done

In this land that we have taken
With the ideals we profess
There's a brotherhood we've squandered
From a past we don't confess

Toward a setting sun we've traveled
Every day since we were born
In the morning light we've waited
For our country's heart to warm

In the courts of inquisition
Where they try the men of dreams
We have caught the tears of heaven
And worn them on our sleeves

As history repeats itself
When will the day begin
We're not plagued by our submission
And haunted by our sin

Where the church of endless war
Leaves its soldiers on a cross
The clergymen of conflict
Count their profit without cost

Where wars between religions
They manipulate for oil
Releasing deeper demons
While the holy water boils

We have gathered at black fountains
Watched the smoking derricks burn
And cast our prayers upon them
Is there anything we've learned

When they call the word of God
Like a curse upon the land
And mortgage every garden
For a fallow business plan

Is there really any reason
To expect a fertile spring
From those who call the season
By the market share it brings

When we will not feed the hungry
Or house them in their need
And we all are on their payroll
Where will the future lead

Can we prime the pump of giving
In the depth of all our hearts
To become the truly living
When our fears we let depart

Where hate is but a weapon
Fear uses to attack
War becomes the refuge
That rides upon its back

Is it endless in its marching
Off these cliffs we clearly see
Or can we nurture back to nature
Sustaining love we all set free

1/20/2017

The Shovel and the Gun

Jehovah calls the poets to the top of the hill
He pours them full of holy with fire and a will
He sends 'em to the valley with all these things
Makes 'em shout it loud in the house of kings

He sends 'em down like Jesus they come back like Job
Sends the tribes of Abe 'gainst the Alamo
Custer strikes Masada from the Jordon road
Then he drops 'em in the desert where the Mormons go

Judas countin' silver at the supper table
Cookin' up a scheme with Cain n' Abel
They brand a line of spirits called Original Sin
Then kill off all the partners and begin again

By a manger in a stable smokin' Afghan hash
Judas in Armani's makin' two stacks of cash
Cain's been drinkin' all night from the Holy Grail
Abel in a grave ain't tellin' no tales

Mao is talkin' politics with Genghis Khan
Negotiatin' test bans of atomic bombs
Brigham's blessin' Mongols on the Temple hill
Babtizin' in abstention till the water spills

Shakespeare's makin' faces from a brand new Ford
Cowboys guns a blazin' in the House of Lords
Broken bit of china in the Queen's right hand
Hamlet with a hammer leads a marchin' band

Hitler in a beamer down in Malibu
Cruisin' to the Beach Boys after Waterloo
Churchill ridin' shotgun on the phone with spies
Goin' out for cocktails under purple skies

Napolean in nappies in a safety seat
Singin' like a wildman out into the streets
Every cop across the heartland drinkin' blood-red wine
Parkin' under bridges with their AKs and 9s

Barbie with her legs up, Ken ain't around
Getting' hot and heavy with Bozo the Clown
Disney at the window takin' copious notes
Ends up creamin' theme parks with his own wild oats

Elvis poppin' pills watchin' Mickie Mouse
Makin' time with Shirley Temple by Walter's house
In a burned out basement after World War Four
Neil Young is chokin' Kafka 'gainst a quantum door

They close a bar in Bombay with a Buddhist priest
Chase cows for fun down alleys   have the karma released
Recite the Book of Mormon in the Taj Mahal
Read Kerouac and Ginsberg on the China Wall

I'm coughin' up a hairball like a Greenwich cat
Askin' Mr. Jones if he knows where it's at
Holdin' up a finger in a heavy wind
When the shit goes down don't you let it in

So honey, honey, honey, it ain't all love and kisses
So honey, honey, honey, those ain't our tasks
It's more a war of roses than a meet the Missus
More flowers on graves and masquerading masks

Meet me at the crossroads   Eden's Highway 61
It's a garden and a jungle
Bring a shovel and a gun

7/28/2016

Sippin' Salt Lake Kool-Aid

Writin' words to music by the tabernacle choir
Talkin' to a psychic in a thong with a wire
Crossin' First and Temple in a sun hot as fire
Watchin' saints with faces dead with desire

Carryin' a hammer and a vampire stake
At a family reunion eatin' angel food cake
Shakin' up a system ain't no mistake
Beatin' on my own heart tryin' to wake

Sittin' by an Orrin with a senate seat
Diggin' on the vibe 'til he gives a speech
Spoutin' party lines but I ain't noddin' yes
People drinkin' Kool-Aid like an acid test

Special interest laws in a Trojan horse
Weakened regulations that they don't enforce
Treat a constitution like a baby wipe
Run it up a flagpole with the stars and stripes

Feelin' like a black man in the KKK
Hosin' burnin' crosses with the words I say
Exposin' party bosses that are on their pay
Diggin' my own grave in the Mormon clay

Tannin' nice and naked on the Great Salt Lake
Cruisin' by the Temple for a beer and a steak
Lookin' for a feelin' that ain't like an ache
Lyin' in their basement is a red rattlesnake

Walkin' in a world made by Arthur C Clark
By Fellini in a beanie trainin' goldfish to bark
There're demons in the semen and they're freed after dark
They're waitin' for Jesus to arrive on an ark

Moses partin' waters in the Great Salt Lake
Gettin' Spiral Jetty tattoos on his coffee break
Zipporah textin' a hook-up sayin' don't be late
Dancin' to the music at the Golden Plates

Josh's blowin' Charlie Parker in the Salt Lake air
Bringin' down the walls in the Temple Square
Rachav's belly dancin' smokin' real good Kush
I'm drinkin' with Jack Mormon in the SugarBush

Droppin' F-Bombs down an alley hear 'em echoed back
Sirens in the distance know it's time to pack
Drivin' to the airport by the river of woe
Liftin' off the tarmac and I'm happy to go

7/30/2016

The Rumble in the Distance

This is how it starts, this is how it starts . . .

A rumble in the distance, a whisper from within,
a current of resistance, your fate upon the wind.

This is how it starts, this is how it starts . . .

Secrets told in private, we've seen it all before,
hate behind agendas, plans made behind doors,
people in high places, multi-nationals with ties,
money, power and influence, campaigns spreading lies,
drum beats in the papers, deals made in back rooms,
threats and accusations, don't anybody move.

This is how it starts, this is how it starts. . .

Storm clouds in the future, gunshots in the night,
division sown between us, hate and fear and blight.
Flags and false diversion, blame and bad intent,
manufactured conflict, the money will be sent.
The boys are in the safe-house. The witness has been paid.
The sniper's in the window. The poison's on the blade.
Self-righteous indignation of privilege and pride,
the prejudice and perjury among the ones who hide.

This is how it starts, people rising from their seats.
This is how it starts, boots marching in the streets.
Truncheons and the tear gas, shields and armored cars,
blood stains on the pavement, people behind bars.
Freedom hung suspended in the belly of the beast.
We know he was arrested, he never was released.
Intention masked as terror, intention masked as crimes.

Innocents are sacrificed, they've done it many times.

People hold the power, this the truest thing.
When taken to the streets, the final bell we ring.
But we've a different story, it strikes us at our core,
The last time that it happened we had a civil war.
There's nothing civil in this, no humanity, no dream.
Turning one against the other is the work of a machine.

This is how it starts, control and marshal law.
Brother against brother, the punch that breaks the jaw.
The fear that kills the spirit, the fear that freezes minds,
The fear for life and family that's with you all the time.
Be brave now as it gathers.
Be brave now as it falls.
Hold it in your heart. Let them hear it in your calls.
This is how it starts in everything we say.
This is how it starts in what we do today.

7/22/2016

Of Armies and Generals

If flags were buried in lost graves
and from them bugles called no reveille
if the words of dead soldiers wrote history
and war held no memory past midnight's armistice
if conflict's profit was made bankrupt by honorable men
and weapons were re-forged into lasting community
then old generals could tend to armies of grandchildren
and perhaps a golden rule for peace could be negotiated
by widows and orphans

12/23/2016

This Much I Remember

I am in the company of soldiers I have
fought beside forever
I am in the company of Red Cross nurses who have tried
to heal my wounds to no avail
I am in the company of enemies I learned to love
in the final moments before I killed them
I am stacking bodies on the fields of battle
I am among the dead
I am among the living

I have been the sound of horror
the thud of flesh and bone giving up
life and blood for something
I did not understand
I have been the sound of anguish
I have been the sound of burning pain
and last rites
I have been the sound of telegrams
and tears

I have been your friend
I have been your brother
I have been the bayonet you feared
I have been the bullet you did not hear coming
I have been marching my entire existence on this plain of war
and this much I remember

my heart was always broken by it

8/8/2016

58

What I Never
Thought to Imagine

What I Never Thought to Imagine

Monastery crows tying ribbons of absolution
to insecure weathervanes and pecking out love songs
on tower bells

Icelandic fog dreaming of warmer seas it had once tasted
on the windblown tips of adulterous waves

Your breath on my ear painting your dreams
in me while we both lay sleeping

Invisible colors flashing in mirrors breaking
my heart and bringing inconsolable tears simply
because they wished to be seen by someone in love

Short-lived emotional dust devils blowing across bone
deserts searching for companionship

Darkness in its passion yearning to reveal a beauty
it was blind to and so drives the night out to live alone

Perfectly folded silk scars infused with the scent of fog
on shuttered windowsills of white beaches never visited

Remnants of memories and unclaimed thoughts left
floating above pillows of day-workers who dreamed poets
and painters took their misspoken words as brush strokes
of inspiration

Homeless love letters asking forgiveness dropped
like thunder from storm clouds over broken homes

An old postman on his last day at work wondering
how he would paint that feeling of disquiet
he had had lately

The last time I would see you
and would I know it

8/18/2016

61

Counting the Ten Small Stones

Ten small stones were in her fist.
She, not more than one or two,
sat like an angel by the path
watched from the distance me and you.

As we came she raised her face
soft as feathers she held my eyes.
Fist extended, fingers down,
she clenched her secret, her surprise.

So I bent to take her gift
offered up my open hand.
She released her blessing there
And dropped it light as ocean sand.

Ten small stones picked from the path,
in her gaze she called to me,
please make sure you noticed them,
look close at what is there to see.

Blades of grass, stars in the sky,
all of heaven's sweet detail
in that moment she revealed it
there beside the garden trail.

Children see what we mostly don't,
the magic in the smallest things.
We want the music made by God,
yet will not hear it where it sings.

Let's go like lovers in this dream
and awake to each new day
to count the ten small stones we find
in everything along our way.

7/17/2016

Mysterious Treasures

For Carol

I have a cousin
who lives in gold country
She sends me treasures
from our mysterious world
    A pound two-pence
    from the ancient kingdom
    A scallop shell from a bay
    north of Barnstable
    A charm in the likeness
    of Confucius
    A royal joker on a bicycle
    And a feather
    from a colonial bird
    as light as air
In my mind I see them
as a perfect mobile
turning in a quiet balance
I am comforted by the image
and sleep a deep sleep
watched over by ancestors
In December's morning
of the second coming
I wake to a new glorious day

12/3/2015

63

It May Be Gone by Morning

This is a harbor town of our east coast heritage.
Across an oil-sheen river of recall night's streetlights
watch each other. Stoic virtues guard a salt-ravaged
bridge between our past and present selves. A full moon
of potential is hidden by clouds of dark thoughts.
A lighthouse beacon scans an ocean where our ships
were once adrift. The wreckage of marriages lie submerged
off cold-shouldered beaches. Bed sheets like torn sails
wash up on yesterday's sharp-spoken rocks.
Old summer homes are abandoned. Whispered regrets
perch on third story widow's walks. Happy hour is over.

All the places downtown love did not go dancing
are still haunted in us. Summer's thunder and lightning
converge where the hill-top cars of spring made love.
Desire's eyes flirt through photos of unkissed lips.
Restless lust paces under a boardwalk and waits for the one
who did not come. The time she left her imprint in the soft
sand and rose the flower in him still holds fragrance.

The places we did not think to look when life's hurricanes
lifted the roof off our optimism are still out there.
Those gloved years that separated the hand of career
from the touch of family can't be counted.
The beaches and summer days are now timeshares
as time allows. With no stake in them they are little more
than billboards along this washed out road.
Morning walks through the gates that used to wave
at the sea. The winter storm-broken arcade piers call
to their buried Junes and Julys, that in its grief August
is trying to forget.

These salt-sea pools remember though.
There are worlds in them. At least they still move with tide
and wind. We were like them once.

Out there is the weather front with its mind-menaced gale.
It carries the promise to wipe this shoreline away again.
I have grown tired of storms and shuttered windows.
All these tourist memories are leaving. The amusement park
will go on state assistance soon.

There is little to do but walk the treeless spit one more time.
It may be gone by morning.
9/6/2016

She Could Find No Tears

She unfolded like
a dry spider
out of her dream

Arose like a dead queen
without a kiss

Stared through the mist
of her tea
to the horizon where
something was missing

In the wet ring of
her cup
she could find no tears

She saw her future
in the settled tea leaves
and went back
to her bed

His ring
at the bedside
no longer round
8/28/2015

The Heat of Words

Showers in the night-bright
full skies   of unabridged   stars
gathered   from the dust
all said and
done

discovered   in the straight
descent   star-shaped
in the aerolite core
feeling   the
heat
          goes
                    falling
                              falling
            through
the   awake
                    and
                         waiting
in   be   tween

to   be   found
in sand   cooling
on the
page

1/30/2017

66

Trust the Melody

We are instruments for makin' music
We are piccolos oboes and violins
We are played in the naked night like harps and drums
We are crescendos and long drawn out moan-like tones
We sing staccato   vibrato   legato
and minor low notes
oh so sharp when we cry

Supple guitar necks bending watercolored strings
into every shade of the blues
Finger-thick sticks beatin' out lyrical licks
What a melody I see you make when you walk
The opera you are owns me
The way you make me hear when
you open your mouth singin' it real
and recallin' those words you heard
These hearts have always been cymbals and bells
I feel the shape of your cello playin' mellow notes to love
Strokin' my ears soothin' my fears

Trumpets and trombones
you are my marchin' band   all brassy
or smooth muted mourns   French horns
Heart and soul music   dream trains   soft refrains
You unlock keyboards of cool   black and white swan songs
Symphonies of a deaf composer's blinding imaginings

And here   these mad minstrels
these moon-dark midnights
all this flesh needin' to dance
with a passion that can penetrate souls with sound
Vibrate like reeds on clarinets   no regrets
Be whole notes lustful in music's trust
Become a melody to renew worlds in all of us

8/26/2016

Eli Is Three

Do you know how big you have to be
for three?
You have to go through
one and two
One and two are hard to do

But three?
Oh, three's as easy as you please
As easy as a hiccup or a sneeze
As easy as a summer breeze
You'll find it so darn easy to be three
More fun to do than two
I'll say that much to you

Three's as fun as anyone
has ever seen
More fun than eating jelly beans
or chocolate creams
You like chocolate or so it seems
Three's like eating chocolate all the time
You'll like it fine

Three's like floating on the wind
or dancing to music you hear within
It's like flying 'cause your trying
wonderful new things
and learning what you couldn't do
when you were two

Three's like magic in that regard
it isn't hard
You'll see
Three's the perfect age to be

7/15/2016

Noah is Six

What wonder, what delight!

Six is discovery.

Six is a deep-sea creature swimming

in your own ocean.

Six is a whole dinosaur buried

in a sandbox .

It's a world with six full moons

where you are king.

Six is a pyramid with a hidden treasure of gold

and only you can find it.

Six is a special friend with new games to play.

Six is a rainbow in a sky without rain.

Six is music you have never heard.

And oh, how you will sing it!

Even from where I am

I will hear you sing.

We will all watch you light up

your candles and step onto the stage of six

where you will sing its new songs

in your bigger voice.

4/19/2017

A Poem Should Be Sharpened

like a penknife

Taken to oiled stone repeatedly

Honed Honed Honed

The edge of it

kept balanced and straight

until at last

razored across the ear

it draws blood easily

7/16/2015

A Poem is the Only Key

When you feel you are locked out,

when I myself am locked out,

when you are broken and cannot heal,

when I am broken and cannot heal,

when the small child in you cries, inconsolable,

when I cry, inconsolable,

a poem is the only key you need.

Remember though, each time one is turned,

and you hear the lock sigh its release,

you must let it go.

When another key is needed, reach for it anew,

until one day there may be

no more doors to block your way.

Then if you can,

turn back and hold them open for others.

8/13/2015

Birthday of the Nine Muses

The old voices are speaking again.

These are not the voices that commanded
Raymond to stand in the center lane at rush hour,
or convinced Kay to stop her meds and walk the canyon edge
at midnight. They're not the voices that told North-side
Norman he could fly from the Burnside Bridge.

These whispers are a subtler form
of madness, no less demanding.
    This mania in heavy traffic,
    this pill of dreams at the abyss,
    this pair of wings over arched waters,
    are a pen as passage home,
    a paper séance on the perilous edge,
    a river rescue under a bridge of words.

Let us search for ghosts where there are ghosts.
And where there are wild borderlands let us run.
Our Gods and monsters will hunt demon-saints
for pleasure. Let's stalk these nights, both vagrant
and homeless, and bask in moonlight as pauper-
princes, kings and queens, incognito.

Call the attendant entities on unseen wavelengths
to these fires where we gather. The fire we burn in,
the light we are and the light we are becoming.
Imagine as you will and we will imagine more with you.

Our dreams are windows. Our dreams are doors.
Become the songs that sing themselves. They will take on lives
of their own, they are our children. Set them free.

This is not just Spring, this is the Birthday of the Nine Muses.
Light the candles and sing the songs of the age we're in.
Let us wage peace and become the voices of children
flying in this new world.
4/4/2017

A Box with Teeth

The Man Who Balanced the World
On the Tip of His Tongue

Tripping is easy he said

It's how you land on your knees

that's hard.

You shouldn't count on too much.

I like to keep my hands busy.

Keep it spinning if you can.

Balance?

Well, I wouldn't know about that.

Just get up as often as you fall.

10/8/2016

Song of the Butter Monkey

I'm just a butter monkey
turn up the heat
Look at the organ grinder
dead in the street

I'm just a butter monkey
let's dance in the sun
The coins of the organ grinder
see what they've done

I killed the organ grinder
went to sleep free
Woke in the morning
with ten more like he

The din of their music
tears up my head
climbing the walls
in a dance of the dead

I am a butter monkey
turn up the heat
I'll melt down a gutter
under the street

Come crank the barrel organ
do it ourselves
The heads of the organ grinders
stacked on the shelves

10/7/2016

Minding the Box

This box has teeth.
I made it myself.
I made myself into
a box with teeth.
I shut the window
in the box with teeth
and I made myself dark
to forget the box.
I swallowed the dark
to forget the teeth
and I could not remember
the light.
And my fear of teeth
became the day
I could not recall
I had swallowed a box
and so made it whole.
I made myself sick
and lay as if dead
and dying inside
I fell asleep.

The I that I am
dreamed I was a box
that could wake
to the light larger
than dreams and bigger
than boxes
where fear, a mere nightmare,
was toothless.
We could love in this box
where I hold the darkness
between my teeth.

10/5/2016

Joan Left Home

Joan left home
with a saxophone
and drove alone
to the streets of Rome
where she was T-boned
by a baritone
wearing headphones
and a moonstone
What was skintight
like a birthright
he a white knight
to her Snow White
became a fistfight
in a bombsite
She got frostbite
had to ghostwrite
in the twilight

In a star-filled sky
she purified
on a mountain high
And by and by
her heart's hi-fi
exemplified
a dragonfly
In the alchemy
she found validity
and velocity
for her majesty
She turned bravery
into rhapsody
and for all to see
set her worlds free

11/2/2016

At the Tables of Words

A dry bone on a fine china plate
Bitter wine in a crystal carafe
Small hard seats   dry wind   hot sun

Whole bread and fishes
bleeding light into a paper cup
Upholstered kingdoms under vibrating stars

We All Run

She wore shot glass earrings
Danced with the synchronicity of geese
Ran like a parody of flamingos

The Dark Persistent

What with this weight goes ankle-deep
and turmoiled beats upon the ears
Midnight's curse abducts the mind
and sings the dirge no other hears

What morning's sun might resurrect
to step deft-toed upon its light
By noon becomes the drumskin skull
tight in torrents   eclipsed of sight

Who would last the heavy years
the pain-pitched battles hidden fought
Dark persistent enemy
covert therein remains uncaught

1/12/2017

Love and the Artist's Calling

Her glazed chameleon heart
her muted palette thoughts
tinted her affections
for the lesser love they bought

She frescoed affectations
buried feelings worlds apart
a host of mawkish passions
galleried like gilded art

Jeweled fears framed the pain
wedding's dust   retreated kings
formed a chain of beggar princes
on their knees with rusted rings

When canvas-covered lovers
like dead muses lined the walls
morning's bed   a still-life portrait
showed no masterwork at all

In the glass of calling's fire
that fuels the vital thirst
she desired by the end
what she'd not been given first

White primer was the mirror
where reflected eyes could see
an ignited airbrush laser
bare what hidden wished to be

She defied blind demons access
to a resurrected muse
struck them dead with her forgiveness
drew a visage strange and fused

From a self-love cup of colors
flamed a beauty so sublime
and from ashes of false idols
she brushed the brilliance of her mind

12/9/2016

Dead Men and Déjà Vu

There are men not buried properly.
There's no going back.
The dead rest best in peace.
I worry the rusted gates
are hard to lock.

Lifetimes stack up and weigh
like too much of everything - heavy clay.
I pace the same old ground digging it up.
My ears ring like church bells.
I experience my morning ritual
and déjà vu with the same ambiguity.

Hard October rain is trying
to tell me something.
It floods the land clean.
I drown in the gentlest memories
when they come back to life.
If there is a reason we die
the rain knows what it is.
It's in the sheer moments
of wonder I feel free.

10/17/2016

Still in the Ribs

                    Faded silk
        shirt on the dresser   Mirrored in the glass
            above   a look   a way   he held himself
            like his chest was a field of broken
                arrows   points buried in
                    bone   A piercing
                      silence echoed
                        no beating
                          heart

He held an empty flask of trips in late-night taxis tarnished
by old neighborhoods with their rain-washed   streets
places he'd torn from a list of forgotten addresses
Wine-stained notes rose off hotel napkins
phone numbers in pointed   feminine
serif on linen   Lovers he recalled
by area code and perfume He
still had their   lined letters
written taut as bow strings
wrapped in a   band of thorns
All collected in small drawers amid
a clutter of cufflinks tie clasps Mason's pins
the mementoes of a father for a child as old as his
broken crystal watches dead to time Crease-cracked
photographs engraved sentiments on worn-down rings
remnants remaining like bloodied fletching   still in the ribs

2/13/201

82

Knowing   Getting   Letting Go

When you knew that the sky had no edges
and you knew by watching the birds
there were places to go
When you knew Alaska was not a small
house in New England
And you knew the top of a mountain
was not a broken church on a desert of belief
When you knew by watching the ocean
that there was mystery in deep places
Then you came to a place of getting

where you thought about getting out
of the cold and into a kiss
You thought about getting to Oregon
and that small house with a garden
You thought about getting a job
You thought children could get you to pray
You thought about getting them shoes
and into better schools
Later you got a divorce
You thought about getting something
from the top of a mountain
where you went to let go and you knew

how to do it by watching the sky
let go of clouds
When your children had children
you let them go
You let the kiss go You let the job go
You prayed and let your prayers go
Your parents grew old and you let them go
On the beaches and the mountains
you held their ashes and let them go
You let them all go into the mystery
of deep places   the next place to visit
3/28/2017

Only Feathers

No matter
what the answer is
about death,
embrace the inevitability
with the rest of your
eternity.
In the remaining time,
build aviaries with roofs
made of sky.
Raise white doves and ospreys.
When a thing cannot be
made better, release it
like one of these.
In the end everything
takes to the wing
and
only feathers fall
down.

9/13/2015

I Hear the Birds Laughing

When I attempt to fly from my troubled heart
When I raise my paltry wings to lift my soul
When I struggle to move against the wind
When I wish for a lighter burden
When I cannot soar even in my dreams
When I wake flightless
in the morning
I hear the birds laughing

9/20/2015

A Season's Songs

John the Baptist by the Pool

Johnny B sat by the pool
The diving board was blue
The country club was wealthy
The clientele were too

All the members came and went
Each had paid their dues
Johnny B taught swimming
At the deep end of the pool

They wore their robes like vestments
Up to the ladder down
But never would relinquish them
And drop them to the ground

Many would tread water
Most held the side of pride
Few swam the laps required
To reach the other side

Johnny B wore sunscreen
He tanned in golden light
While those who feared exposure
Burnt red by summer's night

Dawn found them in their luxury
Windows shuttered tight
While Johnny B woke early
Swimming laps in morning's bright

Johnny B would call to them
With his whistle made of sun
Though every ear could listen
Those who heard were nearly none

Some would float and some would sink
All wished they would be saved
But those who would not wet their feet
Stayed in their safer shade

When Johnny B taught lifesaving
They paid for the profound
Yet they ask to be refunded
When it required them to drown

4/28/2017

Wild Bill's Aces and Eights

Aces and eights
Aces and eights

Men sit at tables where dealers tempt fate
You can't tell the cards by their size or their weight
Five with no faces call death by the date
Bullets in bodies bluff no flushes or straights

Aces and eights
Aces and eights

God makes a world where the devil just waits
So draw from the deck but sit with restraint
The game may be lost by those seated late
You must lay down your hand to tally the slate

Aces and eights
Aces and eights

So remember my friend time's card game kills
And we'll all shuffle papers in Probate and Wills

8/16/2016

Song of the Holy Bones

Let's go down to the river baby
Let's go down right now
I wanna rock these holy bones
Baby won't you show me how
Baby won't you show me how

Baby sell your diamonds
Baby sell your gold
Let's drink up the river
and satisfy our souls

Let's go down to the river baby
Let's go down right now
I wanna rock these holy bones
Baby won't you show me how
Baby won't you show me how

Let's weave a cloth for Satan
from everything we loath
and make them in America
the Emperor's new clothes

Let's go down to the river baby
Let's go down right now
I wanna rock these holy bones
Baby won't you show me how
Baby won't you show me how

Baby sell your diamonds
Baby sell your gold
Let's drink up the river
and satisfy our souls

6/11/2016

The Petals and the Rose

We could walk through lives of fire
With a mind we wouldn't close
If we only could remember
The petals aren't the rose

What the blossom holds like fragrance
Above its stem of thorn
I have nurtured like a birthright
In a world so weary worn

I have picked my child-like garden
From a schoolyard armed stockade
I have been both Cain and Abel
In the choices I have made

There are roses born from passion
There are roses plucked from grief
We forgive them in each other
To render our release

We are vessels of love's power
We're connected to its source
We call it down with glory
Or we will it up by force

We could wake ourselves in Eden
We could do it unopposed
If we only could remember
The petals aren't the rose

8/14/2016

Thunder and Lightnin'

She ain't no easy pickin's
I like to get my licks in
She'll take you down
She'll take you down
To the river

She's like thunder in the distance
She's love without resistance
She'll take you down
She'll take you down
To the river

She's a storm out on the ocean
I need her rollin' motion
She'll take you down
She'll take you down
To the river

She's chemistry
she's alchemy
She welcomes everyman
Refuses charlatans
She's my lightnin'
She's my food
Mess with us
it could get rude
She burns my clouds away
Keeps dark thoughts at bay
She's in the words I say
The final price I'd pay

6/23/2016

Under My Hat

I got white crosses by my bed
Roses and lilies lyin' there dead
I got hard feelin's best left unsaid
I'm growin' a skin I may soon have to shed
Got fires and desires
There's nothin' I require

Got a heart light as air and bigger than such
Got golden ideas worth at least twice as much
Been to my knees where still I keep in touch
I got broken places but not one crutch
Got fires and desires
There's nothin' I require

I got incantations as sweet fascinations
Got bright visions from dark constellations
Guardian angels as love's blood relations
Got only respect for all generations
Got fires and desires
There's nothin' I require

Yet I got somethin' for you babe
What do you think about that
It's hard and it's fine and it's under my hat
Got fires and desires
There's nothin' I require

7/4/2016

Memories of Maine

The Goodwin Roads

Before Longfellow wrote his poems
Before Millay wrote down her odes
Along the pavement we pass over
Our family walked the Goodwin Roads

Long before the Great Maine Fire
Wagons pulled the lumber loads
East of Alfred south of Sebago
Our family walked the Goodwin Roads

At the junction the headstones stand
Men and women with no debts owed
Graced in granite names we carry
Our family walked the Goodwin Roads

Their place in time but for us fades
The story of them near implodes
Save for the few left here to tell it
Our family walked the Goodwin Roads

Swan Pond Creek drains to the Saco
Where our memory now erodes
They gave to life what we now harvest
Our family walked the Goodwin Roads

6/20/2016

We're More Like Smoke

Come my cousins now we've grown older
this life we're living's but a dream
Let's brush these woodchips off our shoulders
nothing we know is as it seems

The cords we've stacked will not pass over
on other's fires they'll shed their heat
and our investments we won't roll over
we'll leave them unburned by the street

The years are felled like hardwoods falling
now deeper forests sing our name
It's in our blood that we hear calling
and in our song that sings no shame

We're more like smoke above these fires
We're more like fire than this wood that burns
in our dreams and our desires
lie things for which our spirit yearns

6/18/2016

Wine and Sacrament

I have eaten live lobster with dying men.
I have steamed in the seaweed-glow of evening
with women and words. I have filled the sails
of ships so long moored they could not plot
a course to morning. I have fallen to my knees
on sand praying for souls drowned and found frozen.
I have shed the tears of seas broken on the rocks
of a heartless time. I have stepped into the fires
of witches still burning.

All these ghosts are with me now. Shift in your seat,
they linger near you. Give them a place at the bar,
they have the greater thirst. Their days are gone.
We now fill their old shoes. Lock-step is lock-step
in any time. Where are the places free souls
can haunt on these shores tonight?

I am a child somewhere in an old house alone.
It is a haunted place, yet I am not frightened.
There were angels then, there are angels now.
They have your family name. You bear their likeness.
They are reflected in every sky and dark water.
They lose no sleep, they are not impatient.
They sing their songs in traffic. They cast their shadows
in the evening fog. They peal no ship's bell laughter.
They tiptoe on buoys and everything drifting.
They ride tides like breathing.

They pause on nights like these. Can you sense them here?
Kindness and softer words are their cup. Companionship
and the held gaze are their grace. The open ear, the open
heart, the open are their door. We are their blessing
and they are ours. We are each other's wine and sacrament
on nights like these.

6/19/2016

Spirits Widow's Walk

Cold coughs its worries in the churchyard
A hard life plows the glacial ways
These stone walls groan the burdens
we stack in our nights and days

Hopeless walks the shipwrecked sands
Hapless drifts upon the tides
A plow horse can't see past his blinders
so plows away his life and hides

In the streets of tight and narrow
Witches' ghosts burn in the chill
alive in death they spirit ever
tied to stakes we carry still

Along these roads we pass each other
as though the other had no name
when a simple smile revealed discovers
there is no other   we're all the same

6/14/2016

Colors of the Brook Trout

Give me the colors
of the brook trout I knew
as a child when late September
called them up into the shallow veins
of the earth to spawn.
Give me the reds and grays,
the haloed blues,
the midnight black,
the fin's milk-white stripe.

Give me the blood of New England
when it flowed clear
in the shadows of hardwoods,
when joy was water
and air
and light
through the trees.
When reds and grays were mystery,
haloed blues were hope,
midnight black was wonder
and the fin stripe was the milky-
white essence of life
and every possibility.

2/27/2012

Omen or a Good Word

Night didn't turn white till the cavalry took Topeka

The trains ran on time years later

Dogs forgot how to talk to crows

Somewhere along the tracks to El Paso

It was a simple language, but it got the job done

Now we try to remember when we walked barefoot

with a full vocabulary

We'd be happy to have any feather fall from the sky

We'd consider it an omen or a good word

maybe an adverb or a pale noun

As words run on sentences

trains run on the tracks of time

Today we'd take the train if it wasn't so slow   and if

it would leave its tracks for the headwaters

where timeshares have opened the sky

You can see Topeka from there   but not Calvary

Night is still white   but that could change

if the word got out

4/24/2017

Charles R Castle Jr was born in Maine in 1951 and has lived in Eugene, Oregon since 1978. His heart is in Oregon. His roots are deep in colonial New England. He worked 27 years in healthcare education and public affairs, with a few years spent in the building trades.

He was published as a young writer in *Hanging Loose*.

After retiring in 2015, he started writing poetry and prose again, publishing two books of poems, *Living with Patriarchs and the Twelve Poems of Goodwin Hatch* and *A Season's Second Coming*. His work has been accepted at *Setting Forth – on a Literary Itinerary* and in a subsequent anthology *Poems on Poetry and Poets* published in 2016.

It is in the shared resonance of the spoken word he finds inspiration and community.

Minutes Hours and Days was published in *Poems on Poems* by SettingForth - -on a Literary Itinerary.

Only Feathers
I Hear the Birds Laughing
A Poem Should Be Sharpened
A Poem is the Only Key
She Could Find No Tears
On Winter's Death
are reprinted from *Living with Patriarchs and the Twelve Poems of Goodwin Hatch* - a distribution of 100 copies completed in 2015.

Made in the USA
Lexington, KY
19 May 2017